MOTHER DEUCE™

by George Poppel

Tennis Etiquette and the Rules of the Game

MW01242298

MOTHER DEUCE

by George Poppel

Tennis Etiquette and the Rules of the Game

Illustrated by Everfever

PANDA MONIUM BOOKS

Inprint Books
P.O. Box 12184
La Jolla, California 92039

Copyright © 2021 Inprint Books, P.O. Box 12184,

La Jolla, California 92039.

This book is dedicated to my two beautiful granddaughters,

Caroline and Isabel.

Do you want to be king or queen of the court?

Tennis is the nicest of sport.

Etiquette is always the rule.

Walk on someone's court and you'll be considered a fool.

It is not the most important thing to win

To see who goes first you must spin

Your racket, while your opponent calls up or down

If you lose the spin, please don't frown.

You must call the lines fairly

To win a point squarely

Even if the ball merely touches the line

You must call it in and please don't whine.

First, you must learn how to keep score.

This is not a very difficult chore.

The first point is fifteen

The second point is thirty

Next comes forty

The fourth point is game.

CHAMPIONS TOURNAMENT

CAROLINE GREEN

ISABEL BLUE

Now, to win a game you must win by two points

Forty all is deuce

It is like a truce

All sides being equal

Then comes the sequel:

The server's point is add-in,

The receiver's point is add-out.

Then it is either game or deuce.

CHAMPIONS
TOURNAMENT

SABEL BLUE

CAROLINE GREEN

40

40

At deuce you keep playing until someone

wins two points in a row.

This is a very important rule to know.

The first player to win six games wins the set.

Then the players should all shake hands at the net.

But you have to win by two games.

At six-all, you play a twelve-point tie-breaker.

The first one to seven points is the winner.

As long as he or she wins by two

Keep it up until you are through.

Winning is not the most important thing.

Good competition should make your spirit zing.

It is better to lose than to make a bad call.

Tennis etiquette is being gracious and fair above all.

The End

Made in the USA
Middletown, DE
18 April 2023

28913640R00015